MOVING ON...

'Healing through verse'

A book of poetry

By

Lee Taylor-Friend

Published by High Country Press
P.O. Box 946
JINDABYNE NSW 2627
Ph: (0408)166-200
www.leetaylorfriend.com

PHOTOCOPYING
Please keep in mind that photocopying threatens the viability
of future re-prints. Please help our small press by recommending
this book.

PURCHASING
Please see our website www.leetaylorfriend.com and click on
purchase for a list of stockists. e-mail: leetaylorfriend@hotmail.com
or call (02)6456-7310 or (0408)166-200.

National Library of Australia Cataloguing-in-Publication Data:
Creator: Taylor-Friend, Lee, 1968- author.
Title: Moving on...Healing through verse.../Lee Taylor-Friend.
ISBN: 978-0-9944290-0-1   (Paperback) First Edition
ISBN: 978-0-9944290-1-8   Print On Demand - CreateSpace
ISBN: 978-0-9944290-2-5 E-Book
Subjects: Healing--Poetry. Dewey Number: A821.4
Text typesetting and design by High Country Press and Blizzard Publishing
First edition printed in Australia by Blizzard Publishing, Jindabyne,
Snowy Mountains.

Cover illustration by Jan Owens
Cover design by Kerry Beer Photography
Proof read by Jean Gamon

Disclaimer
All care has been taken in the preparation of the poetry herein, but no
responsibility can be accepted by the publisher or author for any
damages resulting from the misinterpretation of this work.

Dedication...

For John, Ben, Jake and 'Jinda' Jean Gamon.
Your unswerving love,
support and laughter
inspire me to work towards
healing, creating and
being the best me I can be...

Acknowledgements

To everyone who has supported, inspired and encouraged me.
Thankyou...
To Verity and Libby for your sage advice and friendship...
To Kerry and Jan for your amazing artistic flair...
To those on your own healing journey,
'May the love and light
of a million hearts and stars
guide your way...'

MOVING ON...
FOREWORD

After much soul searching this book has come to fruition.

It is raw – personal – honest. For some it may be confronting.

For me it is a culmination of ten years work on many levels.

I believe that by speaking our truth we allow others to do the same.

Life is not always 'a bed of roses', as is evident in this book of poetry, but we can 'move on' if we don't bury the past and close the door on healing.

I believe 'writing as therapy' can be such a positive tool for growth and renewal.

This is well supported by research and literature.

I ask people in my workshops to dig deep and reach a place of truth.

I will not ask of others what I have not asked of myself.

Below is an excerpt of a testimonial from one of my workshop attendees – I will leave the last word to Heather...

"Lee's workshops are ostensibly about writing and the fact that everyone has their own unique story to tell, but they also subtly encompass psychology, philosophy and some very valuable life lessons.

The direction her teaching takes is shaped by the students, as I have observed by attending these in different communities.

It takes a lot of skill and understanding to be so adaptable, and to make each student feel that they have something worthwhile to offer and say.

My writing quality and self-understanding have been moved forward exponentially by what I have learned from Lee, as have the other workshop attendees that I have maintained contact with.

I would not hesitate to recommend Lee's workshops to any potential employer – they will get more than they bargained for in a very positive and healing way."

Love and light...

Lee Taylor-Friend

<u>MOVING ON…</u>
<u>NON-CONTENTS PAGE</u>

It has been a deliberate decision not to number the pages in this book and to have a 'non-contents' page.

An act of literary anarchy if you like…

In all honesty it is about time and numbers.

How often are our lives ruled by them??

Have you ever found yourself saying 'I'll just read for ten more minutes and then I have to…' or I'll read page one to five before I rush off to…'

How about start at the beginning and finish at the end or reverse it and work your way backwards!

Stop where you will – use a bookmark or not – the choice is yours…

Start, finish, savour, reflect, in your own time, own space, no limitations, just words, time, warmth and love…

Yours in verse

Lee Taylor-Friend

MOTHERLESS DAUGHTER

So many years have passed now,
Since Mum chose not to stay.
Why is the pain and grief so raw?
Will it ever go away?

I miss the brief encounters.
My memories so few.
Many a day I cry and grieve,
For the Mum I never knew.

I was just a babe in arms,
When the 'big depression' came.
You were sick on and off for so many years,
But none could heal the pain.

The drugs, shock treatment, 'therapies',
Did not seem to help.
Nor your doctor, who by all accounts,
Could have done with some healing himself…

I will never forget that morning,
Our Aunts, they came to the door.
The loss and the pain etched in their face,
Nobody needed say more.

We sat and hugged and cried and cried,
Until no more tears could come.
For never was there a sadder day,
When a child loses their Mum.

But life goes on, you must be strong,
For your family and yourself.
But it's always there, like a cross to bear,
You will question your own mental health.

Years have gone by, time has passed,
Now I am a Mother too.
At times I do miss achingly,
A Mother that I barely knew.

Now I know a Mothers' love,
So strong and true and free,
It makes me feel somewhat at peace.
I hope that's how you felt about me…

For I am a 'Motherless Daughter',
It's my legacy you know.
But few will ever see the scars,
The ones I seldom show.

The silent pain, the tears that fall,
To see them will be rare,
For I am a 'Motherless Daughter',
It's my story that I share...

I REMEMBER...

I remember conflict.

I remember Pain.

I remember Sunshine.

I remember rain.

I remember family.

I remember friends.

I remember love and loss and ends.

I remember you my love, my friend.

3.13AM
(SLEEPLESS IN JINDABYNE)

Sleeplessly

I trawl

Through the multitude

Of thoughts

Echooooing through my head.

A plethora

Of pontification

A maelstrom

Of mind fodder

All vying for paper space…

Try to sleep

Though

As I may

As I should

I can't.

I write

I think

I plan

I dream

But awakenly so…

So much
To do
Yet
So little time
To do it.

In less than three hours
Master three and a half
Will awaken
With his usual
Unbridled enthusiasm.

My maternal hat will
Firmly replace that of
The self-indulgent writer
With some reluctance
Yet irrefutable relief.

SIXTEEN STOREYS
MEMORIES OF REDFERN

Sixteen storeys.
Families piled on top of one another.
Lives in a box.
A huge oblong sixteen storey block
With inter-connecting hives
We all called 'flats'…

'803' was our number.
The blue flats.
'Lawson' they were called.
Three sixteen storey
Monoliths - all in a row
Named after poets…

The significance of this was
Lost on me as a child
I just knew them as the
'Yellow'
'Red' and
'Blue' flats…

The local clutch of shops
Was most originally known as
'Poet's Corner'.
I never
Saw anybody
Reciting poetry there…

Everyone too engrossed in the
Machinations of life.
Lively gossip.
Goings on. Survival.
General chit-chat
Of life…

They seemed overwhelmingly
Enormous to me as a child
Yet upon re-visiting them
As an adult
More akin to small
Secular pigeon holes.

Funny how time changes perception…

I looked out the window
Where a man once jumped.
I remembered many times
Being kept inside by
Mum and Dad
Because 'someone had fallen'…

I recalled watching
Fireworks at the old Easter show
Lying, belly down, on cool concrete
Peering wide eyed under the railing
Too vertically challenged
To see over the blue painted metal …

I remembered Mum, when she was well,
Cooking crumbed lamb cutlets.
Dad bringing home the obligatory
Bottle of 'Sparkling Rinegolde'
On a Saturday night
In a lifetime so, so long ago…

<u>NOT HERE…</u>

A certain kind of sadness

Fills my being.

I pretend not to know why

But I do

It's you.

Your birthday today

But you are not here…

Your voice and

Laughter linger

But you are not here…

Your features

So prominent on

Your grandsons face

But you are not here…

Tears streak the paper

On which I write

But still, you are not here…

THE EBB & FLOW OF LIFE
(BOXING DAY 2004)

I was lying down just resting, but I could not get to sleep.
My head was filled with memories, so personal and deep.
They do well up from far within, the feelings that we keep.
The memories that we do sew, and those we sometimes reap.

The news it said a big wave came and took them from the shore,
300,000 lives lost but perhaps its many more.
They say the Lord he giveth and he also takes away,
As I close my eyes, remembering, and for their souls I pray.

It's hard to know what one could do, I stared in disbelief.
The pain etched in the faces, the bitter smell of grief.
The homeless and the orphaned, the children meek and mild.
I've seen the pain of those who lost their Mother, Father, Child.

When such a horror happens we think what's it all about?
Those who have so very much and those who are without.
Give thanks for every day we live, for every breath we breathe.
We may not know it's coming, when it comes our time to leave.

Forget about the trivial, have grace each day we can.
Respect and love our children and embrace our fellow man.
I guess there is no one answer and we all must do our best.
Give what we can to make sure all are sheltered, fed and dressed.

Send all our love, our thoughts, our hope,
To ease the pain and strife.
We pray that time will quickly heal
The 'ebb and flow' of life…

THE LAST GOODBYE...

The winds of change are blowing,

I feel it in the air.

A certain kind of knowing,

Finality to bear...

I watch that subtle swaying,

Gentle rustling fills the breeze,

Fading slowly to the distance,

He leaves, He leaves...

THE MESSAGE

Melancholy falls

like a misty cloak

covering me

in a veil of uncertainty.

This is the way

it has been for years,

coming and going

at will.

I have learnt

not to question it.

In time it passes

and I am released.

A lonesome cork

bobbing

in a longed for

sea-of-calm

as the storm battered bottle

sinks deeper, deeper,

to a foreign ocean floor

with an unknown

message inside.

THINK ABOUT ME

Sometimes I'm feeling so alone,
This sweet serenity.
Sometimes a heartache overcomes,
That only time can free…

Sometimes I'm feeling life's so sweet,
Sometimes I walk and fall.
Sometimes I'm in a no-man's-land,
No comfort there at all…

Sometimes I wish to spread my wings,
To soar away on high.
A songbird pure and wild and free,
Embraced by endless skies…

Sometimes I feel forgotten,
No matter how I try.
I'm giving all I have to give,
The thought can make me cry…

So look within my heart and soul,
And tell me what you see?
I'm always here to comfort you,
So babe just think about me…

You see I'm always there for you,
You know I'll always be.
Sometimes I need some comforting,
So babe just think about me…

THE RIVER WHISPERS…

Your ancient wondrous wisdoms

As you guide me through your land

Are whispered on the gentle breeze,

Immersed in river sand…

The echoes of the spirits past

Are calling out to me

Reminding me to follow

And fulfil my destiny…

But what is it? This destiny?

This path that I must travel?

'Be patient' voices whisper

For in time it will unravel…

HOW DO YOU EVER SAY 'GOODBYE?'

So many years together,

Now the time has come to part…

Laughter etched into my memory,

Teardrops falling on my heart…

All the times we shared together,

It was such a magic ride.

Now it seems the journeys over,

You're no longer by my side…

Still I feel your hands upon me,

Catching every tear I cry…

Hearts and souls entwined forever,

How do you ever say goodbye?

How you loved me in the springtime.

Held me in the summer rain.

Watched the autumn change approaching.

Then the long cold winter came…

In time perhaps the pain will fade away,
Release and melt my frozen heart.
I'll think about the good, the happy times,
Somehow I'll make a brand new start...

But for now I'll just remember,
Endless tears I cannot hide.
I close my eyes and see your smiling face,
Fading on the ocean tide.

Still I feel your hands upon me,
Catching every tear I cry...
Hearts and souls entwined forever,
How do you ever say goodbye?

How do you ever say goodbye...?

FOUR TRUTHS @ SIX LIES...

Loss, love and uncertainty.

Constant themes that

Resonated throughout a childhood

Filled with anguish and joy.

Trips to foreign shores on charted yachts.

Unchartered waters – turbulent - vivid aqua.

Foam spilling over the sides

Then calm – just calm...

CONTINUANCE...

My Friend was abused...

Gouging wounds through the psyche and soul.
A sea of life running through.
Weeping stories of loss.
Permeating the DNA of generations.

My Friend is brave...

Clawing at creativity as a cure.
A settler of the nerves.
A healing pilgrimage.
Peace and hope the eventual destination.

My Friend is funny...

Laughter, tears, stories.
Past, future, present.
Metamorphasising as a
Distant drum echo's soundlessly.

Safe travels my Friend...I am on the journey with you xx

SOMETIMES…

Sometimes I'm strong.

Sometimes I'm weak.

Sometimes I'm quiet.

Sometimes I speak.

Sometimes I laugh.

Sometimes I cry.

Sometimes I live.

Sometimes I die.

Sometimes

I just am…

SYLVI...

I think of you often.
The depth of your pain.
Your loss palpable...

Erika.
Not just another suicide statistic.
Your baby girl – gone.

Sister – Daughter.
Friend – Lover.
Life flame extinguished.

Charred ashes and lost dreams...

Sam and Sylvi.
Surviving Sister – Surviving Mother.
Moving forward – Looking back.

A two-woman army.
Brave, Bereaved.
A long, slow journey.

May the love and light
Of a million stars and hearts
Guide your way...

WHO KNOWS...

Who knows what the future holds?

As our destiny unfolds…

Why we choose a certain path.

Fires burning, scorching hearth.

Still, we travel as we must.

True to heart, in soul we trust…

THEY DON'T CALL IT 'DOPE' FOR NOTHING...

I wish I could take away your pain.

The dullness in your heart.

The lividity of your soul…

I would take a machete of gleaming steel

gilded with love

and cut you free from the mindless shackles

that bind you to a life of perpetual misery.

Lies, deception, self-absorption.

The by-products of this 'smoke haze of illusion'

as pythonic manipulation surreptitiously

squeezes the life out of those around you.

"I'm fine! I'm fine!" she says.

"It's everyone else that has the problem."

They don't call it 'dope' for nothing…

COMPLEXITY @ CONTRAST

Rain @ misery

Sunshine @ joy

Pride @ passion

Girl @ boy

Lovers @ dreamers

Husband @ wife

Friends @ family

This is life…

FOR SARAH...

Life is full of ups and downs

Magic moments - chilling sounds

Mystery permeates, surrounds

On this enduring journey...

Rivers flowing - banks and bends

Heart connections know no ends

Love and laughter shared by friends

On this enduring journey...

Change and challenges we face

Loss, acceptance, grief and grace

Across the globe we still embrace

On this enduring journey...

MOVING ON...

"I didn't hurt you – I never would hurt you…"

Your opening line at my Fathers' funeral.

You made a bee line for me and spoke these words.

It told me so, so much…

My Father's funeral.

Not the time or place

to de-construct the complexities

of a relationship that was.

At such a young age I came to you.

A new start – A new hope.

But things don't always work out.

No Brady Bunch ending here…

There were positives – don't get me wrong.

But for years the memories of verbal put downs

and fear of physical retaliations

is what stuck with me.

Fear…

Half the time I didn't know what I did wrong.

Maybe a hyperactive child who wanted

love and a deep connection was just

too much with the other demands of life present and past.

It took me years to heal from the pain.

Your words wounded far more than your hands.

Years later I understood - you had your own scars and suffering.

Your unresolved pain started the cycle again...

I am no longer angry. I got over that long, long ago.

I have healed. I have a good life.

I hope you find peace. I hope you find happiness, contentment, joy.

I hope you find you. We all deserve that...

AN UNEXPECTED GIFT...

The water tank kangaroo hopped in front of me.
I was about to yell "Get off that damn bobcat before you hurt yourself".
My words never got the chance.
Instead your scream tore through the green plastic.

"My leg, it's f#cked, I'm f#cked..."
My vision obscured – I ran to your side.
Our eyes burnt into one another.
Fear their wordless message.

I looked down.
Not brake fluid but blood pouring out of your leg.
Bones smashed, splintered.
Flesh torn apart.

Hidden by blue denim.
I was thankful for that.
Even through your blood loss and grey pallor
You were braver than I.

"Is Daddy going to die??"
Our sons' honesty spurred me to action.
"No. Daddy will be O.K."
What could I say...

Tourniquet – towels – must stop the blood.
Phone calls – Friends – 000.
Re-enforcements on the way.
Assessments made – Helicopter called.

Early evening gave way to dark.
Airlifted to Canberra – into the unknown.
Vibrations – Operations.
Inclinations of grief over valour.

"Will you save my Leg?" you asked.
"Yeah – we'll put it back together"
Doctor 'Blue Shoes' in Emergency said.
Not sure if they were suede…

Commuted. Crushed. Compounded.
Surrounded by carers
Coercing bones back to uniformity.
Encouraging flesh, grafting, crafting, the best they could.

It looks like a shark bite some say.
"Yeah, I was surfing Waimea – 30 foot waves -
The Great White came outta nowhere…"
"Sick of the bobcat story" you laugh.

Several years have passed since the accident
Blast through our lives,
Into our psyche and out the other side.
You have taught me much about much.

Positivity, Humour, Acceptance.
"Sh#t happens, you can't change it,
You just have to deal with it".
Your words of wisdom…

Time.
Reflection.
Introspection.
Your accident was…

An unexpected gift.

<u>2010</u>

Year of transition, year of change.

Year to adapt, to re-arrange.

Year of challenges, year of pain.

Year of learning, year of gain...

Introspection, reflection

Growth and visions anew

As two become one

And one becomes two...

Year draws to a close

But the lessons stay longer.

'What doesn't kill you,

Makes you stronger...'

ASPI®E…(For Ben)

Two sons – two gifts.

One 'Aspie' – One Neuro-Typical.

But what is typical?

What is normal??

The diagnosis helps 'neuro-typicals' to understand 'Aspies'.

I suspect 'Aspies' would need a tome

From Sydney to Rome

To understand 'Neuro-typicals'.

We are all different.

Learn differently.

Love differently.

Acceptance is the key.

A key that will unlock a room of beauty,

Peace, diversity – emerald encrusted,

Gilded with wit, wisdom, laughter.

A place beyond our imagining…

THANKYOU…

Once again I stood on the edge of reason
looking over the abyss.
A little too close to the edge this time.
I lost my footing and fell…
Not far albeit.
Strong ledges were there,
glaringly close to the top
to break my fall.

Our friends and family are these ledges.
They help us on our way,
clambering back up the
rocky slopes of life.
The ones who share our journey.
Who listen, sympathize, understand,
accept, acknowledge, identify,
support, nurture and care.

The two largest rocky outcrops
have gone from my life.
My Mother, my Father.
But in their place are many smaller,
incredibly important stone ledges
of immense strength and comfort,
joining to make a smooth path
back to safe and solid ground.

Thankyou for leading me home…

COLOURS

What colour am I? She asked.
I thought about that question a lot…
I hope it is not too presumptuous
Or overambitious to say…
I think I am all the colours
Of the rainbow these days…

It was not always so.
But then who is to say,
A rainbow is not there
In the night, after day?
Is it that we cannot see it
When the darkness falls??

A new day dawns.
Light emerges.
We can see our rainbow
For what it truly is
A unique, magical,
Beautiful thing!

Perhaps it was there the whole time…
You just seem to notice it
That much more,
Coming out of the dark of night,
And into a beautiful,
Brand new day…

And isn't it funny how other people
See the beauty of that rainbow
Well before you ever allow yourself to…
Black contains all the colours
Of the spectrum - It is white that reflects them!

DECONSTRUCTION OF A HYSTERECTOMY...

Farewell my uterus.
Seat of my womanhood.
Nurturing - life giving - womb within.

Elimination of my ovaries.
Seeds of life.
Created twice.

Hard to fathom - comprehend.
Emotion overwhelms and sticks.
A hysterectomy/oophorectomy at 46.

Logical side takes over.
Complexities - Family history of the big 'C'
Can't hide the fear – danger lives here…

Time to go – it has to be.
No more kids on my dance card.
Still it's hard…

Farewell and thank you.
You have served me well.
On April Fool's Day, you will be gone…

VISION AND VALOUR...

A professional face is what you see,
But underneath there is me,
I observe, I feel, I hear, I decree,
Empathy, intuition, acceptance must be...

So much love, sorrow, joy tempered with loss,
Strength, sadness, laughter, tears,
I feel them all,
Not mine but I feel them...

A double-edged sword - My strength? My weakness??
But is it a weakness to feel, to intuit???
I will not put up a wall to emotion.
That is poison to my soul...

Contemplation, acknowledgement, honouring the cycle of life,
Stories, memories, humour,
Radiating for perpetuity,
A privilege to share, to care...

In private I too have my tears.
Not for death, but for life.
Not for loss.
But for humanity...

VISION...
RISK...
COMPASSION...
HARMONY...

These words of wisdom you shared.
I shall honour them, as I honour you...

PEACE

As transient as it may be

when it comes

it embodies a completeness,

a calm, a palpable serenity

that fills the soul with an understated

sense of bliss.

Oh how I long for you to be in my life

on a more permanent basis.

Not an elusive stranger,

but a comfortable companion.

But would life be anywhere near as

interesting?

Would my words dissipate like

a virgin dew on a hot summers' morn

for lack of inspiration???

Still, a little more peace would be, well,

Peaceful…

Life

Life changes so quickly.

A tsunami

of epic proportions

can come and wash away

everything you know

and trust

leaving hearts

and homes

scattered and broken...

The clean-up.

Change.

Transition.

A new kind of new.

Challenging old ways,

old beliefs.

The journey that is life...

Growth.

Resurrection.

Sometimes good.

Sometimes bad.

Acceptance.

Then more change.

The only constant...

TRUE WORDS...

When I was a girl of nine or ten
my Father used to say
"If you don't love yourself no one else will".
I'd laugh and run away.

As I navigated teenage years,
self-esteem dropped through the floor.
"If you don't love yourself no one else will".
He'd repeat it more and more.

As I blossomed into adulthood
I appeared so self-assured.
To the outside world I was doing fine
yet internal demons roared.

The words Dad said seemed somehow vain
"love yourself" – a strange concept.
Sometimes I'd see the shining light,
then the flame of self-doubt leapt.

A man can love you true and deep.
A childs love swell your heart.
Friends and Family love, support
but what happens when you part?

You can be in a room of a thousand friends
yet somehow feel alone.
To understand, embrace, accept,
love internal must be grown.

It's taken years to live these words,
before I could truly say,
'I love myself' and in doing so
can love others more each day.

The seed of love when grown within
will envelop, flourish, thrive.
Enriching those around you.
Keeping love and hope alive...

UNDER THE PERMAFROST...

Under the permafrost she lies.

Frozen, still, waiting.

Observing.

Sucking in air and life

Through a hazy, mottled view.

Frozen but still learning.

Ice cold droplets awaken her knowing.

The sun is coming.

Defrosting her soul.

Cool waters gush over her.

She is comfortable,

Comforted by her nakedness.

Her back arches.

She rises.

Up, up into the light.

WHAT WILL YOUR FOOTPRINT BE???

There's a consciousness arising,
an awakening of the soul,
as the people come together
to achieve a vital goal…

Awaken from the apathy,
complacency and see.
Protecting what we have today
may change our destiny…

Look forwards, yet glance backwards,
at the lessons of our past.
It's time to learn, move on, evolve,
this world is turning fast…

In an age where greed destroys the earth,
the very air we breathe.
Such disparity t'ween social classes,
racial tensions seethe…

We must have a 'social conscience'.
Extend a helping hand.
If to 'give is to receive',
then let's protect this sacred land.

For money can't buy happiness
or truth or clarity.
We are on this earth to change it so –
WHAT WILL YOUR FOOTPRINT BE???

WORDS...

Trying to find the answers,
To the questions still unknown.
How my thoughts, my happiness,
My challenges have grown...

To share such things, provocative,
So pure and some in haste,
Telling of my memories,
No precious time to waste.

A problem shared, a problem halved,
Or so some people say.
I never thought I'd find my peace,
Or solitude this way...

It may not always resonate,
You may not quite agree.
Some might find it poignant,
Might bring tears or set you free.

To some it might mean nothing,
These words that I impart.
It doesn't really matter,
It's just coming from the heart...

The 'Writing as Therapy' works...

In August 2015 I was engaged to create and present a series of three workshops focused on writing as therapy for Carers ACT.

It was a wonderful series of workshops to facilitate.

A remarkable group of Men and Women to work with.

I found it a highly creative time and share with you on the next few pages the various 'August 2015' poems I wrote or, as I like to refer to them, the 'Writing as Therapy' works ...

Mind Dump 7/8/15

Sounds rude doesn't it!!

Whatever comes to mind
Is relevant, O.K.
Express and feel, think, reveal
It's where I am today.

A group of carers, sharers,
So much to explore.
I hope they learn with wisdom,
Open a new door…

It is a new life journey.
Sometimes nerves abound.
I flush a bit and sit and think
And then I look around.

Writing, exciting!
Exploring a new world.
Evolution, solution to
Some of life's complexities.

It is an honour to be here.
To share, explore and write.
End of poem/paragraph.
Thank you and goodnight!!

Rainy Day Letter to Self...

I love you.

I would never have said that
Five years ago,
Two years ago
Six months ago, But I do…

Why do we find
Those three words
So easy to say to others
But not to ourselves??

Even when I hated myself, I love you.
I reflect back on those times
Of self-doubt, self-hatred.
I shower them with love...

They have all led me to
Where I am, to who I am.
I am grateful for the hard times.
They have built strength, resilience, determination.

I am grateful for the great times!
There are plenty of those
If we choose to look.
I am grateful for this life…

Expressive Letter to Others...

Thank you all.

Everyone here
Today
Tomorrow
Yesterday
But especially today...
Thank you to my Family.
My three boys
Who fill my world
With love,
Music,
Wonderment.
Thank you nature.
Trees.
Grass.
Dew.
Sky.
Rain.
Dirt.
Earth.
Thank you for the marvel
That is nature.
Thank you for allowing me
To notice it from time to time.

Thank you for it all...

This Day…14/8/15

This Day…
What I observe around me,
Astounds me.
Surrounds and envelops me in
Learning and wonderment.

Life is a journey
Never-ending, bending,
Ebbing and flowing,
Going to…
Who knows where next.

A text,
From my son,
'Good luck Mum with
your workshop today'
'We Love You…'

More precious than
Money,
Possessions.
Family, love and giving,
The greatest gifts of all…

THREE SPRINGS…Spring One…

New life,

New hope.

An explosion of imagery.

In multiple hues.

Warmth,

Comfort,

Sheep poo collected

In buckets and

Mulched into

Garden beds.

The vegies will come.

The fauna will fornicate.

Spring is here.

YIPPEE!!!

Slowly new life awakens

Plantings thrust through the ground

Romance abounds

Igniting passion

New life

Growth and renewal

THREE SPRINGS…Spring Three…(The Spring)

I did not realize

How important

It was until

It was gone…

Time stopped.

My life in disarray.

When would I work?

When would I play??

Then…

A realisation

dawned.

Freedom, Freedom!!

The spring had sprung.

My watch kaput.

A tiny spring,

Squished underfoot.

'Don't call me late

For dinner'

He says.

Well now I can…

Reach Out…(For Jake)

History is littered with stories
And happenings gone wrong.

Give me your ear and your heart
As I sing my sweet song.

Live for the moment with
Truth, love and fine clarity.

Honest and strong, fair to all,
With the hope to be free.

Reach out your hand,
Just one touch and the truth will be told.

'Love conquers all' is the message
That shall not grow old.

Pages for you...

These last few pages
are for you.
To write, create
and reflect too.
Don't be afraid
Just start to write,
Creative sparklers
Will ignite
Then rouse and stir
Your brilliant brain.
Let me repeat
This true refrain.
Don't be afraid
Just start to write!
Trust your internal
Guiding light.
Just have a go.
Release the strain.
Fare well
Until we meet again...

The final word...

Thank you for taking the time to read my book.

May writing become your Friend.

A supportive companion in a complex world...

<u>Pages for you…</u>

Pages for you...

Pages for you...

<u>Pages for you...</u>

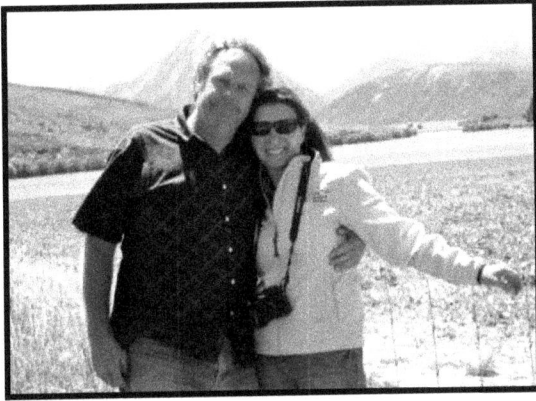

<u>MOVING ON...</u>

Lee Taylor-Friend is a Mother, poet, writer, support worker and remedial massage therapist living in the picturesque Snowy Mountains region of Australia with her husband and two sons.

She also creates and presents writing and poetry workshops where she shares her love of the written word and passion for 'writing as therapy'.

Lee has been widely published, won several awards, has a popular monthly column in the Snowy River Echo and volunteers her time for a variety of community events, local committees and causes.

"Moving On..." is an honest, thought provoking and moving collection of poetry that is deeply personal.

This collection of verse is the first of several diverse books of poetry Lee plans to release as both paperbacks and e-books in 2016/2017.

www.ingramcontent.com/pod-product-compliance
Lightning Source LLC
Chambersburg PA
CBHW060722030426
42337CB00017B/2961